ANCIENT EGYPT

Troll Associates

ANCIENT EGYPT

by Laurence Santrey

Illustrated by Hal Frenck

Troll Associates

Library of Congress Cataloging in Publication Data

Santrey, Laurence.
   Ancient Egypt.

   Summary: Describes life in ancient Egypt and the
accomplishments of that advanced civilization.
   1. Egypt—History—To 332 B.C.—Juvenile literature.
[1. Egypt—History—To 332 B.C.]   I. Frenck, Hal, ill.
II. Title.
DT83.S25   1985   932'.01   84-2728
ISBN 0-8167-0248-9 (lib. bdg.)
ISBN 0-8167-0249-7 (pbk.)

More than 10,000 years ago, small groups of people settled along the Nile River in northeastern Africa. They were descendants of prehistoric hunting tribes that had wandered over the continent in search of food. At the fertile banks of the Nile, the land was rich and green. And the plants growing near the river yielded seeds, which they ate.

In time, the settlers learned to plant the seeds and grow new crops of food. From these simple beginnings came the great civilization we know as ancient Egypt.

The early inhabitants of ancient Egypt developed many skills. They sewed and wove cloth and reeds. They made clay storage jars to hold grain, oil, and water. They were adept at hunting and fishing and successful in raising animals for food and work.

The key to the good life in ancient Egypt was the Nile River. Every year, the Nile overflowed, flooding a wide strip of land in the river valley. When these summer flood-waters receded, they left behind a deposit of rich soil called silt.

This fertile, black soil enabled farmers to produce a steady supply of food, and made possible a civilization that would last for thousands of years. In fact, the ancient Egyptians called their food-giving land *Kemet*, which means "black," for the rich, black soil.

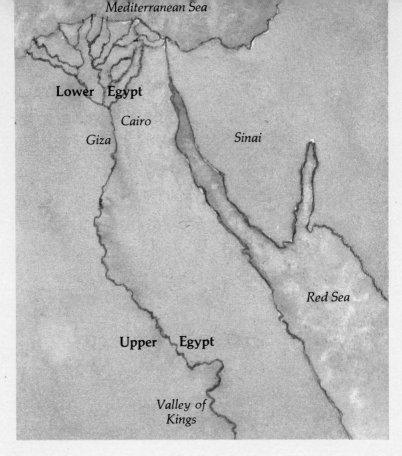

Mediterranean Sea

Lower Egypt

Cairo

Giza

Sinai

Red Sea

Upper Egypt

Valley of Kings

In time, the tribes that lived along the Nile united into two kingdoms. These were called Lower Egypt and Upper Egypt. Lower Egypt included only the low, swampy land of the Nile Delta, near the Mediterranean Sea. A delta is a triangular section of land at the mouth of a river, and it is formed by deposits of rich silt. Upper Egypt included the land that lay south of the delta, along the banks of the Nile.

About 5,000 years ago, Upper and Lower Egypt were united by a king named Menes. This marked the birth of the great nation that enjoyed splendor and glory for more than 2,500 years. From this point on, the history of ancient Egypt can be divided into several time periods, each including one or

more dynasties. A dynasty is a succession of rulers from the same family.

The first period of ancient Egyptian history is called the Early Period. It began with the reign of King Menes and the dynasty he founded. And it came to a close 400 years later, at the end of the second dynasty.

During those 400 years, Egyptian civilization took giant leaps forward. Writing, in the form of *hieroglyphics*, was introduced. Hieroglyphics are written symbols. But they are not an alphabet. Only some of the hieroglyphics stood for letters. Others stood for whole words. And still others stood for entire ideas.

The ancient Egyptians left many records of their civilization written in hieroglyphics. These picture symbols have been found on clay tablets, on paperlike scrolls of papyrus, on the bases of statues, and on the walls of temples. But modern people didn't know what the hieroglyphics meant until a little more than 100 years ago. This was when the writing on the Rosetta stone was deciphered.

The Rosetta stone is named for the place in Egypt where it was found. On it were three kinds of writing—Greek letters, hieroglyphics, and hieratic writing, which is a short form of hieroglyphics.

Using the Greek letters on the Rosetta stone, scholars were able to work out what the hieroglyphics meant. We still do not know exactly how the Egyptian language sounded when it was spoken. But the Rosetta stone has made it possible for us to read the words of the ancient Egyptians.

During the Early Period, Egyptians also learned to use metal tools, to study the heavens, and to develop systems of arithmetic. From their study of astronomy and arithmetic, they were able to create an extremely accurate calendar.

The Egyptian calendar had a 365-day year. It was divided into twelve months, each of which had thirty days. The five days left over were used for religious celebrations. The Egyptians also divided each day into twenty-four hours, a system which continues to this day.

The next period in the history of ancient Egypt spans about 500 years. It is called the Old Kingdom, or the Age of Pyramids. The pharaohs, or Egyptian kings, were very powerful rulers. The Egyptians believed the pharaohs were gods who walked the Earth. They also believed that all the land belonged to the pharaoh. In return for being allowed to live on the land, the people had to pay taxes and work part of each year for the pharaoh.

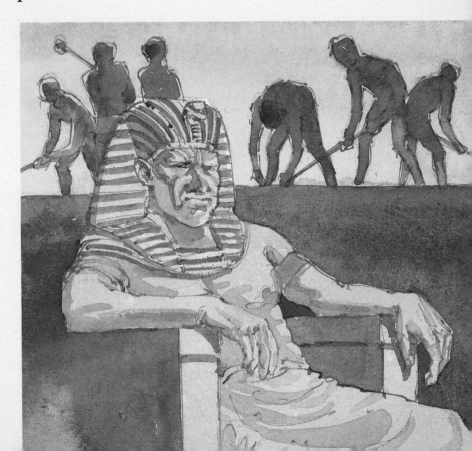

During the Old Kingdom, much of the labor and taxes went into the building of the pyramids. The pyramids were huge tombs built for the pharaohs. They were also monuments to the greatness of the pharaohs. Egyptians believed that life did not end with death. They believed that the spirit of a person continued to exist forever. The solid majestic pyramids were ideal for guarding the pharaoh's body and the soul it contained.

The largest pyramid of all—the Great Pyramid—was built for King Khufu. It took many years, almost all of the national treasury, and more than 100,000 workers to build it. When it was finished, the Great Pyramid held more than two million blocks of stone and covered thirteen acres of land.

During the Age of Pyramids, more than twenty major pyramids were built. They were the largest structures on Earth and were considered among the great wonders of the ancient world.

A large stone lion with a human head was also built during the Age of Pyramids. It still stands today and is known as the Sphinx.

The third period of the history of ancient Egypt lasted about 150 years. It was marked by civil wars and a decline in trade and culture. It was not until about 2050 B.C. that peace and stability were restored.

During the fourth period, called the Middle Kingdom, Egyptian trade flowered anew. Egyptians brought back gold, copper, ivory, marble, and jewels from various parts of Africa and the Middle East. They exported vases, combs, and other finely crafted products. They built beautiful palaces and stone systems for distributing water. And they produced a wealth of art and writing during this time.

It was a rich and fruitful period for three of the four classes of Egyptian society. At the top was the ruling class, made up of the pharaoh, his family, the priests, and the nobles. The next class was made up of merchants, craftsmen, and traders. Below them were the workers, who labored in the fields or the cities. At the bottom of Egyptian society was the class that never did well. It was made up of slaves, who were mostly foreign captives brought back to Egypt by merchants and soldiers.

After more than 200 years, the prosperous Middle Kingdom came to a close. During the next period, rulers grew weak, and Egypt was invaded by fighting tribes, called the Hyksos, from Asia. The Hyksos used bronze weapons, armor, and horse-drawn chariots to defeat the Egyptians. Finally the Hyksos were driven out, the Egyptian economy was strengthened, and the New Kingdom began.

One of the pharaohs of the New Kingdom was a woman—Queen Hatshepsut. Her reign was a peaceful, productive time for the

country. It was also a time when many handsome temples and monuments were built. Among these were the tall, thin pillars of stone called obelisks. The obelisks, covered by hieroglyphic writing, were erected to honor the sun god, Ra. They may also have been used as giant sundials.

After Hatshepsut died, her name was scratched off the monuments she had built. Her stepson, Thutmose III, became pharaoh, and he wanted her memory erased. Unlike his peaceful stepmother, Thutmose was a warlike pharaoh. He sent his armies south and northeast, expanding ancient Egypt to its greatest size.

Another important pharaoh of the New Kingdom was Amenhotep IV. A wise and peaceful man, he introduced a remarkable idea called *monotheism.* Monotheism is a belief in one god.

Until this time, the Egyptians had worshiped many gods. But Amenhotep

worshiped only the sun, which he called Aton. He changed his name to Akhenaton, which means "pleasing to Aton." Claiming he was the son of Aton, he forced everyone to worship him as a god-king.

During the reign of Akhenaton and his queen, Nefertiti, the arts, sciences, and mathematics flourished in Egypt. It was a time of peace and plenty at home. But much of the outlying land—land that had been conquered by Thutmose—was lost during the reign of Akhenaton. Finally, after his death, the Egyptians returned to their old religion, worshiping many different gods.

Akhenaton was succeeded by his son-in-law, Tutankhamen. King Tutankhamen, or King Tut, was not a very important pharaoh during his short lifetime. But his tomb, which was not discovered and opened until the twentieth century, has made his name well known to the modern world.

King Tut's tomb held a treasure of gold and jewels, as well as the untouched mummy of the pharaoh. There was also a miniature boat to ferry the dead king to the afterlife, plus food, games, furniture, and anything else he might need there.

The tomb of King Tut had stood for many centuries, undiscovered and untouched. Tombs built by other pharaohs had been discovered, opened, and looted by grave robbers long, long ago.

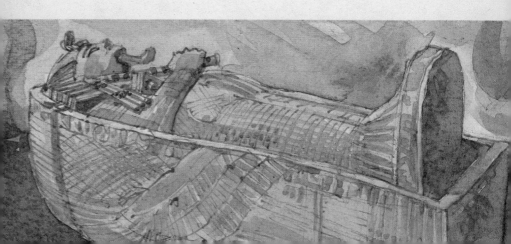

After the death of King Tut, ancient Egypt again expanded, and for about 200 years, held a position of importance in commerce and trade. When the New Kingdom ended, the Egyptian Empire had become little more than a group of separate states without a strong central government. Although it continued for another 1,000 years, ancient Egypt had passed the peak of its greatness. Other civilizations had become more powerful.

During the Period of Invasions, they began to take over sections of the Egyptian Empire. Over the years, Egypt was conquered by the Libyans, the Sudanese, the Assyrians, the Persians, and the Greeks. In fact, the Ptolemies—the last family of pharaohs— were originally Greek, rather than Egyptian. The last member of the Ptolemy dynasty was Queen Cleopatra. When she died in 30 B.C., Egypt became a colony of the Roman Empire.

The sun had finally set on the great civilization we know as ancient Egypt.